# Anne Wolkodaw

# Information Management

# Anne Wolkodaw

# Information Management

## How to deal with
## the information paradox
## in business' daily life

VDM Verlag Dr. Müller

Bibliografische Information der Deutschen Nationalbibliothek:
Die Deutsche Nationalbibliothek verzeichnet diese Publikation in der Deutschen
Nationalbibliografie; detaillierte bibliografische Daten sind im Internet über
http://dnb.d-nb.de abrufbar.

Copyright © 2006 VDM Verlag Dr. Müller e. K. und Lizenzgeber
Alle Rechte vorbehalten. Saarbrücken 2006
Kontakt: info@vdm-buchverlag.de
Coverbild: www.photocase.de

Herstellung: Schaltungsdienst Lange o.H.G., Berlin

ISBN-10: 3-8364-0159-2
ISBN-13: 978-3-8364-0159-3

*to Mr Sven Oppel, the Euro - Business - College Jena*
*and, above all, Mr Brian Ferris.*

# Contents

Page

List of figures.................................................................................... III

List of tables..................................................................................... III

List of appendices............................................................................. III

List of abbreviations .......................................................................... IV

1    Aim of this work .......................................................................... 5

2    Background and key terms............................................................. 6

    2.1    Data – Information - Knowledge ............................................... 6

    2.2    Management..................................................................... 10

    2.3    Costs and benefits ............................................................ 11

        2.3.1    Costs ..................................................................... 11

        2.3.2    Benefits ................................................................. 12

3    Fundamental principles of information management....................... 13

    3.1    The information paradox ..................................................... 13

    3.2    Definition of information management.................................... 15

    3.3    Tasks of information management ........................................ 16

4    Information Economies and Data Flow .......................................... 19

    4.1    The Management of Information Economies ............................ 19

    4.2    Data flow management ....................................................... 20

        4.2.1    Overview................................................................. 20

        4.2.2    Information requirement analysis ................................ 21

            4.2.2.1    Key term, objectives and background ..................... 21

            4.2.2.2    Procedures ............................................................ 23

            4.2.2.2.1    Background ..................................................... 23

            4.2.2.2.2    Subjective procedures ...................................... 24

            4.2.2.2.3    Objective procedures........................................ 24

             4.2.2.2.4    Mixed procedures ............................................ 25

        4.2.3    Communication requirement analysis ........................... 27

            4.2.3.1    Key term and background..................................... 27

            4.2.3.2    Methodology ........................................................ 29

    4.3    Concerns......................................................................... 30

        4.3.1    Information quality ................................................... 30

4.3.1.1    General criteria ..................................................... 30

4.3.1.2    Criteria of information for management ..................... 31

4.3.1.3    Systemisation of information quality........................... 32

4.3.2    Information security...................................................... 32

4.3.2.1    Background and aim ........................................... 32

4.3.2.2    Measures to protect information .............................. 33

4.3.3    Storage of information ................................................. 34

4.4    Evaluation of the optimisation ............................................ 35

4.5    Management Information systems (MIS)................................. 39

4.5.1    Definition and background ............................................. 39

4.5.2    Tasks........................................................................ 41

4.5.3    Operating on different levels ......................................... 41

4.5.3.1    The need for different levels.................................. 41

4.5.3.2    The levels of a MIS ............................................ 41

4.5.3.2.1  The personal information system (PIS) .................... 41

4.5.3.2.2  The work group information system (WIS) ............... 42

4.5.3.2.3  The organisational information system (OIS) ............. 43

4.5.4    Further parts of a MIS.................................................. 44

4.5.4.1    Decision Support Systems (DSS) ............................ 44

4.5.4.2    Knowledge Systems (KS)...................................... 45

5    A optimisation of data flow for art decor® ................................... 46

5.1    History and business of the organisation ............................... 46

5.2    Data Flow analysis........................................................... 47

5.2.1    Preface concerning methodology..................................... 47

5.2.2    Analysis and recommendations....................................... 48

5.2.2.1    Organisation and communication structure................ 48

5.2.2.2    The main office ................................................. 49

5.2.2.3    Chain stores .................................................... 51

5.2.2.4    Stock and inventory............................................ 54

5.2.2.5    Sales at mall events........................................... 54

5.2.3    Implementing a MIS? ................................................... 55

6    Conclusion ..................................................................... 57

7    Appendices ................................................................. LVIII

8    Literature.................................................................... LXVI

## List of figures

Figure 1: Forms of information ............................................................8

Figure 2: Knowledge pyramid............................................................10

Figure 3: relationship of information demand, supply and requirement.....22

Figure 4: balanced scorecard ...........................................................27

Figure 5: communication process.......................................................29

Figure 6: Relationship among components of MIS ................................40

Figure 7: Categories of OIS...............................................................43

Figure 8: Communication structure ....................................................48

Figure 9: Example new calendar........................................................50

Figure 10: a stock related MIS ..........................................................55

## List of tables

Table 1: comparison of tasks ............................................................16

Table 2: tasks of IM........................................................................17

Table 3: procedures of information requirement determination ..............23

Table 4: examples of communication media ........................................30

Table 5: systemisation of information quality......................................32

Table 6: benefit matrix....................................................................38

## List of appendices

Appendix 1: Users manual questionnaire ...........................................LVIII

Appendix 2: Questionnaire...............................................................LXII

## List of abbreviations

BSC : Balanced Scorecard

CEO : Chief Executive Officer

CSM : Chain Store Manager

DSS : Decision Support System

IPS : Information Processing System

KS : Knowledge System

MIS : Management Information System

OIS : Organisational Information System

PIS : Personal Information System

SME : Small and medium sized enterprise

WIS : Workgroup Information System

# 1  Aim of this work

Some things are as they are and they have worked well all the time. People are used to them. Sometimes they know, that things could work better, sometimes they don't.

One important thing in small and medium sized enterprises is communication and the flow of information. This sometimes can be crucial to the surviving of such firms.

Although, some organisations know that they have a deficit in the communication or information process, they are not able to initiate any change.

This work has the aim to point out this critical issue and to show how practices of communication and data flow can be improved.

Firstly, the author gives an overview about theoretical approaches and than she will analyse the dataflow for a commercial organisation of the middle class.

Here, it is important to say, that the measurement of the effects of such an optimisation is hard to realise, as effects can't be measured on numerical or monetary scale.

The main concern of this book is not the theoretical explanation of types of data banks or the programming of such a data bank, which common literature describes. It is rather the establishing of more efficient methods to deal with the daily business and at least not to loose the basis of business, namely, the delivering of value to customers.

Therefore, this work will present a probably total different perspective of this theme in practice, because of the individual tailoring, adaptation and transformation of theory to a practical solution.

# 2  Background and key terms

## 2.1  Data – Information - Knowledge

First of all, it is very important to mention that the three terms listed above are not equal, although, in common language they seem as they were.

But by looking deeper into this subject matter and comparing leading literature it is obviously that data becomes through a process of transformation firstly to information and, as main aim, finally to knowledge. By that it is important to examine these terms in an explicit way to show differences.

<u>Data</u>

Schwarze (1998, p.24) states that data is just information which can be transformed and displayed with the help of technology.

In comparison with other authors this statement seems to be insufficient and superficial. Krcmar (2005, pp.14-15) therefore, identifies data as a combination of single signs or characters or numbers that are part of any alphabet. These single signs have qualitative or quantitative character and are not connected to any coherent statement. They have no context (Eppler 2003, pp. 19-20). A simple example for data is the number 1.43 or the word "dollar".

<u>Information</u>

The information itself has its origin in the Italian language. "informare" means there "educate" (http://de.wiktionary.org/wiki/Information, 14.04.06).

If data is connected to any coherent statement, the resulting entity builds a piece of information. In other words, several pieces of data form the message, which is called information (Eppler 2003, pp.19-20).

Furthermore, information can be an inquiry or a clearing up (Heinrich 2005, p.7).

By that, if 1.43 and dollar is connected in relation to 1 Euro, the data makes sense.

Königer et al.(1998, pp.65-66) defines information in two different ways. Firstly, information is structured. This means that it can be processed in the meaning of business management science, e.g. accounting information. Secondly, those which can be not processed in this way are, therefore, unstructured.

As Krcmar (2005, pp.18-19) identifies the following characteristics of information:

- Information is an intangible asset
- Information provides advantage
- Information is not free and may create costs
- Value of information depends upon its quality, time related use and context
- Information can be shared

A schematisation of forms information gives the following plot:

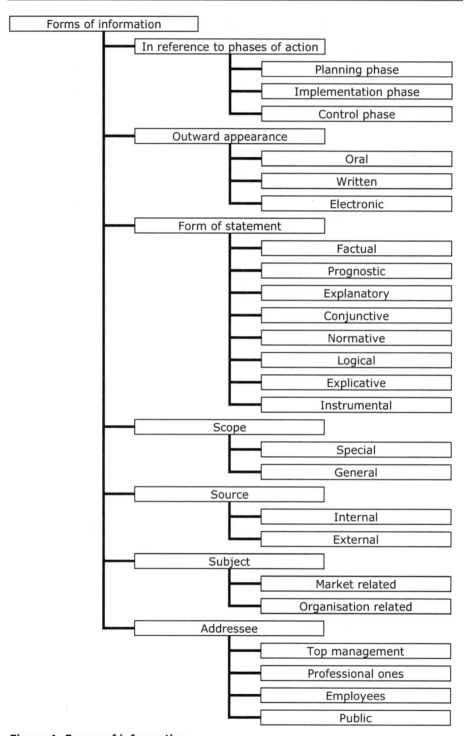

**Figure 1: Forms of information**

(Schwarze 1998, p.92)

Respecting the diplomas object, the author takes up Königers (2003) view that information can be treated as an object, which has content but also meta-information, which can be seen as information about information, e.g. a cover of a CD or a headline of a table, which provides information about the music stored in the CD. By that it is easier to describe the processing of data flow.

<u>Knowledge</u>

The last stage of transformation of signs to data to information is knowledge.

By that, knowledge is not only the totality of information as Schwarze (1998, p.24) states. Rather, it is the connection of information in a coherent way. It is integrated and interpreted in the prior knowledge (Eppler 2003, p.20).

Davenport et al. (1998, p.5) enlarge the term of knowledge "as framed experience, values, contextual information and expert insight that provides a frame work for evaluating and incorporating of new experiences and information".

Another interesting view is the differentiation of knowledge by Nonaka et al. (1995, p.59). They divide it into tacit and explicit knowledge.

Tactic knowledge is strong related to a person's commitment. Therefore, it can be hardly formulated and communicated. It is said, that it is absolutely subjective. It contains the worlds past, current and future view. Skills and capabilities are included there, too. Tacit knowledge becomes visible through acting.

Explicit knowledge can be formulated and systemised. It can be stored, processed and transferred in different media.

Königer et al. (1998, p.68) classify information and explicit knowledge at equal level.

To visualise the relationship between sign, data, information and knowledge the model of a pyramid is most appropriate:

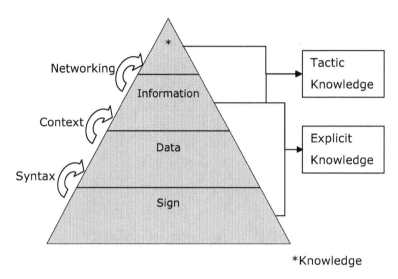

*Knowledge

**Figure 2: Knowledge pyramid**

(own development)

## 2.2 Management

This word has its routes in the Latin term "manum agere" (http://de.wiktionary.org/wiki/Management, 14.05.2006) which can be translated as "leaded by hand".

This leads directly to the problem which this term includes. It is correct to state that management is subject to administration to generate best output (Heinrich 2005, p.7). But in some literature management is equal to leading only, which is superficial. Krcmar (2005, p.23) divides the term into two different directions.

Firstly, management is considered in a functional context. It describes tasks and processes which further can be divided into personnel function and line function. Personnel function copes with the administration of human resources, integration of staff or the arrangement of the work place. Line function deals with the fulfilment of tasks which contribute to the achievement of organisational objectives. Planning, organising, implementation and controlling are focused. These processes are executed on all levels of the organisation, on a low level e.g. a secretary plans (sometimes unconscious) in which order she fulfils her tasks of the day, than she organises issues to facilitate the implementation (e.g. to file the post by importance). Then, she implements her tasks and at the end, she controls that she didn't forget something.

Secondly, management is seen as institution. This institution consists of people, who are policy-makers, concerning line and personnel tasks. Such institutions can be boards and leadership on corporate, business and enterprise level. Most important, regarding to management as institution, are rather the tasks and the competences managers have than their hierarchical position.

## 2.3 Costs and benefits

### 2.3.1 Costs

The subordinate concept of costs is the term of expenses. If expenses are not related to the ordinary operating procedures they are not treated as costs and named as non operating costs. Expenses always reduce the amount of equity (Schmolke et al. 2006, p.354).

In economics, operating costs are the quantitative usage (kg, but also time) or legally obligated pays. Costs need to be valued with a certain amount of money (Schmolke et al. 2006, p.354).

If the amount of costs is dependent on the output, science speaks of *variable costs*. Costs which occur independently from the produced output and are stable in there amount are called *fixed costs* (Detsch 2006, cited in Microsoft Encarta 2006).

Economic science distinguishes also *historical* and *opportunity costs*. Former are recognised in accounting, latter describe the amount of difference of values of two opportunities, where not the best opportunity was chosen (http://en.wikipedia.org/wiki/Cost). E.g. if the entrepreneur invests 100.000 € in ordinary shares of the XXX AG and sells them one day later for 102.000 €, he has earned 2.000 €. If he had chosen the opportunity to buy shares of ABC AG he would have earned 3.000 € by selling them one day later. Therefore, the opportunity costs of buying shares of XXX AG were 1.000 €.

## 2.3.2 Benefits

Benefits or profits describe the evaluation of the success of the company (Kraus 2006, cited in Microsoft Encarta 2006).

Subordinated benefits are always measured in the amount of money in which they increase the equity. Science also distinguishes between operating and non operating benefits. Further are e.g. turnover or capitalised services. Latter are e.g. tax abatements (Schmolke et al. 2006, pp.355).

Sometimes it may be difficult to evaluate success with a certain amount of money. If this is the case, effects should be evaluated by the usefulness they add to a process or circumstance.

# 3  Fundamental principles of information management

## 3.1 The information paradox

The paradox

A paradox often is characterised as a simple contradiction. But the difference between a paradox and a contradiction is that one of two assumptions must be wrong if it is a contradiction, and if it is not, both assumptions can be true, although it seems they can't.

The development of society in industrialised nations generated such a paradox, namely, though there is so much information that there is not enough of it.

To much information and the issue of reasoning

Information is all over there. Regarding to the definition of information above, it must be.

Information transport messages, but what aim do they have? In daily life this could be to entertain people, to educate them, to inform them e.g. about the weather or news, to avoid growing of a traffic jam or to stimulate their buying behaviour. In business life this could be to cause an order because coffee run out, to fill a human resource gap because a secretary is ill or to react quickly because a rival made a better offer to a high potential prospect.

The problem of too much information, therefore, can be identified through external and internal constraints.

The external influences are not only defined trough the mass of information which flows towards the individual, it is also the fact that the same or nearly equal information is provided by too many emitters and this information is repeated. Furthermore, which is most worth, information is provided irrespective it was desired or requested. This fact called Shenk (1997) as "datasmog".

The internal constraints are subject to the human being. De Wit et al. (2004, pp. 52-57) state that reasoning is influenced by three issues: cognitive abilities, cognitive maps and cognitive activities. As cognitive maps are characterised through tacit knowledge or can be compared with a computers running system it is more interesting to examine cognitive abilities and activities.

Cognitive abilities can be compared with a computer's hardware. This means firstly that a human being sensing abilities are limited. While the senses of touch, smell, taste, hearing and seeing are bombarded with information or stimuli, much of it remains unrecognised. The human being is not able to realize everything. Secondly, its information processing capacity is limited, too. By that, not everything what a person realize can be interpreted. To avoid an overload, the human being has to weed useful information out. Finally, not everything what has been processed can be stored. Nearly everything may stay in short term memory, but not everything may stay in mid term memory and just a little bit of the whole will stay in long term memory.

Cognitive activities, therefore, can be compared with a computer's software. Before conceiving and realizing a problems solution, the problem must be identified and diagnosed. To do this in an efficient way the software must be provided with correct and relevant information.

To relate it more to business, it is to say, that management has to be provided with the information which is not only relevant rather presented in an easy interpretable form. By that management may work more efficiently and effective.

<u>Too few information</u>

As there is on the one hand too much information as stated above there is on the other hand often not enough of it.

This means that some information has not been acquired or is not available when needed. This is illustrated by comments like: "This you should have known!", "If I had known that...!" or by daily time kidnapping recherché work, where colleagues are asked, data banks or filings are searched. But also structured research needs time and, therefore, money. Sometimes missing information is used to excuse failing.

As these examples show, not only the missing of the information itself leads to insufficient supply of it, but also its availability. What value does information have, if it can not be used, because it wasn't available at the right time?

Viability of any organisation is dependent on the availability and supply of information, which is necessary to manage processes and human resources.

The paradox explained above, leads to the constraint of establishing information management to use information as production factor and to create competitive advantage by using it in an effective and efficient way.

## 3.2 Definition of information management

To come to an appropriate definition of information management (IM) in context to the diplomas aim, it is necessary to compare several views of it, firstly.

Schwarze (1998, pp. 41), therefore, collected the following different meanings:

- IM as a synonym for commercial information systems
- IM as the management of documents, books and journals, which is near to library science
- IM as the management of information resources, which has a strong connection to computer science management and the using of soft- and hardware
- IM as the management of data, which means the development of data banks and to ensure data security by the use of special information processing systems
- IM as a special management task containing all activities of acquisition, processing, storing and offering of information. Therefore this meaning includes strategic and operational tasks.

With those meanings he came to his personal definition of IM:

> "Information management contains all management tasks (leading, planning, co-ordination and controlling) of the acquisition, processing, transferring, storing and offering of information to support the achievement of the organisations objectives."

Krcmar (2005, p.49) defines IM as follows:

> "IM is the management of economies of information, information systems, information and communication technology as well as holistic leading tasks.
>
> ...IM is a discipline of management as well as a technique and is an elementary part of leading an organisation."

Concerning the diplomas theme, the author agrees with booth definitions, but stresses the data flow management as support function of management's decision making process.

## 3.3 Tasks of information management

Firstly, it is important to mention how varied this topic in literature is. Schwarze (1998, p. 64) compared 13 different authors with 13 different views of tasks of IM:

**Table 1: comparison of tasks**

|  | Biethahn et al. | Frenzel | Griese | Grudowski | Heinrich | Hildebrand | Krcmar | Martiny/Klotz | Österle et al | Pfeiffer | Rauh | Seibt | Zahn/Rüttler |
|---|---|---|---|---|---|---|---|---|---|---|---|---|---|
| Strategic tasks | X | X |  | X | X |  | X |  |  |  | X |  | X |
| Tactic tasks | X |  |  | X | X |  |  |  |  |  | X |  |  |
| Operative tasks | X |  | X | X | X |  |  |  |  |  | X |  | X |
| Information economies |  |  |  | X |  |  | X |  |  |  |  | X |  |
| Management of technologies |  |  |  | X |  |  | X |  |  |  |  |  |  |
| Management of information processing systems (IPS) |  |  |  |  |  |  | X |  |  | X |  |  |  |
| Leading tasks |  |  |  |  |  |  | X |  |  | X |  |  |  |
| Hard- & software systems |  |  |  |  |  |  |  |  |  |  |  | X |  |
| System life cycle |  |  |  |  |  |  |  |  |  |  |  | X |  |

| | | | | | | | | | | | |
|---|---|---|---|---|---|---|---|---|---|---|---|
| IPS concept | | | | | | | | X | | | |
| Architecture | | | | | | | | X | | | |
| IPS project portfolio | | | | | | | | X | | | |
| IPS projects | | | | | | | | X | | | |
| IPS care | | | | | | | | X | | | |
| Strategy/networks/controlling/ personnel | X | | | | | | | | | | |

(Schwarze 1998, p. 64)

This table could be updated regarding to Kcrmar (2005, p. 34), who distinguish different approaches of IM. One of these approaches is the task orientated approach in the German speaking region and is, by that, referring to Heinrich (2005, pp.73-314), who divides the tasks of IM in strategic, administrative and operative tasks.

Schwarze (1998, p.65) amplifies each of those and adds analytic tasks. This scope of tasks, he defines as core tasks of IM. A whole overview of these tasks could be plotted on a grid as follows:

**Table 2: tasks of IM**

| Strategic tasks | Administrative tasks | Operative tasks | Analytic tasks |
|---|---|---|---|
| • Strategic situation analysis<br>• Strategic objective planning<br>• Development of strategy<br>• Strategic planning of implementatio n<br>• Quality management<br>• Technology | • managing projects<br>• Personnel planning management<br>• Data management<br>• Life cycle management<br>• Process management<br>• Knowledge management<br>• Security management | • Production management<br>• Problem management<br>• User service | • Analyses of information requirement<br>• Situation analysis<br>• Organisation analysis<br>• Identification of demand for rationalisation<br>• Innovation management<br>• Market watching of hard- and |

| management | • Management of | | software |
|---|---|---|---|
| • Controlling | catastrophes | | • Analysis of |
| • Revision | • Contract | | communication |
| • Outsourcing | management | | demand |
| • HRM | | | |

To evaluate this table in a critical way, the author mentions, that IM rather is the base to fulfil these tasks efficiently and effective than IM has the task to match all these fields of business.

Schwarze (1998, p.68) rebuild this table by the outsourcing some tasks as cross sectional area tasks. These tasks bother the core tasks and can be seen as support to them, which contain the following parts:

- Data management
- Personnel management
- Security and catastrophe management
- Juristic issues
- Quality management

Regarding to the diplomas theme, the author will concentrate in the continuing text regarding to Schwarze (1998, pp.87) on some parts of the analytical tasks or regarding to Krcmar(2005, pp.51) to Management of information economies.

# 4 Information Economies and Data Flow

## 4.1 The Management of Information Economies

The management of information economies is a core task of the IM. It derives from the statement that information and communication can be seen as production factor and, therefore, information is an asset (Heinrich 2005, p. 223).

Unlike informatics, which deals with the data processing, information economies focus the human being and the satisfaction of his information needs (Encarta 2006). Its aim is the equilibrium of information in the organisation (Link 1982, p. 285).

Moreover, its aim is to acquire data of existing data resources and exploring new sources of data. These data should than be produced in an adequate way, so that it reproduces reality in a way that it responds to the required task (Heinrich 2005, p.223)

Tasks

The global task is to ensure that information is delivered to the right addressee at the right place at the right time in the right form (Schwarze 1998, p.223) in the right amount and in the required quality (Krcmar 2005, p.55). Schwarze further adds the congruency of information supply, demand and requirement, which refers to the information paradox.

Krcmar (2205, p.51) states the following differentiated tasks:

- The balancing of information demand and supply
- The accommodation of decision making management with relevant information
- Guarantee of high information quality
- Documentation of development and implementation of will
- The designing of information economies as supporting task of IM
- The usage of information technology
- Optimisation of timing of data flow
- The concerning of the economic principle

## 4.2 Data flow management

### 4.2.1 Overview

Data flow management is described in general in a very technical way, which is less concerned about which information flows from which point to another point, rather which person involved in business needs which information. The original data flow comes from the development of compilers in the data processing science (http://www.software-kompetenz.de/?21059, 03.06.2006).

The data flow management, here, deals more with the tasks of the management of information economies. Furthermore, it is concerned about data relevance. Data flow analysis has the aim to clear up the information paradox and to structure data flows in small and medium sized enterprises (SME).

Methodology

As literature mostly offers technical solutions rather than practical ones, the author will pick up only a few ideas of it in order to be able to develop a concept for a SME.

## 4.2.2 Information requirement analysis

### 4.2.2.1   Key term, objectives and background

Information requirement analysis is the first main concern of the data flow analysis and copes with the question which information out of the information supply and the information demand is substantial. This implies that it also looks at the information supply and the information demand.

Often information demand and information requirement are set equal, but this is wrong. Information requirement is the information which the task or objective concerns and, therefore, is very objective. Information demand is subjective, because it is that what the recipient of the information thinks is task related (Schwarze 1998, p.88).

This leads to the constraint, that if not all relevant information is demanded, there will be an undersupply of information and if more than the relevant information is demanded, there will be an oversupply. This situation is transferable to the question of information supply.

In practice under- and oversupply of information demand and information supply are present at the same time, which refers to the above described information paradox.

Critical here is the determination of the information requirement. This is because every supplier of information provides information which he thinks it is relevant. Therefore, the author suggests involving a non-partisan third, which helps to clarify the relevant information.

Schwarze (1998, p.89) distinguishes between the individual and global information requirement.

Latter covers the information which is necessary for an optimal achievement of set goals of the organisation as a whole under consideration of available resources.

Former can be described as the information required from a single post to fulfil its task in an optimal way. Moreover, it comes to the fore, because the global information requirement is the aggregation of all individual requirements.

Plotting information requirement analyses gives the following graphic:

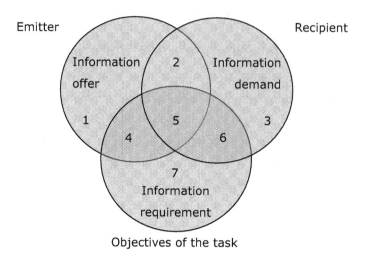

Emitter      Recipient

Objectives of the task

**Figure 3: relationship of information demand, supply and requirement**
(Schwarze 1998, p.92)

The numbers meanings are the following:
1: supplied information, which is neither necessary nor demanded
2: supplied information, which is demanded but not necessary
3: demanded information, which is neither necessary nor supplied
4: supplied information, which is necessary but not demanded
5: supplied information, which is demanded and necessary
6: demanded information, which is not supplied but necessary
7: necessary information, which is neither demanded nor supplied

According to Schwarze(1998, p.91) the forms of information explained above, can now be diversified to a more practical content:
- Information leading to action/information no leading to action
- Periodical/non-periodical information
- Documented/non-documented information
- Organisation internal/external information
- Past/future related information
- Top management/management/operative information

The frontier between top management, management and operative information is not fixed rather floating.

## 4.2.2.2    Procedures

### 4.2.2.2.1   Background

In general, there are a lots of procedures suggested in literature. As the systemisation of Krcmar (2005, pp.61) gives a well structured overview, it will be further explained.

First of all it is necessary to determine which person needs which information. In contradiction to Krcmar, the author states that the only involvement of a third non-partisan party to determine required information is insufficient. This is because not all information identified by the third party may be useful and necessary in practice. By that, also organisation internal persons should be involved.

All parties involved, than should be pooled in different groups and be used as objects of the examination of information requirement. Those groups of example can be stakeholders, employees, decision making management, customers or consultancies.

Now there are three different kinds of procedures:

| Subjective procedures | Objective procedures | Mixed procedures |
|---|---|---|
| • Open interview<br>• Wish catalogues<br>• enquiry of third | • Strategy analysis<br>• Process analysis<br>• Input-process-output analysis<br>• Decision analysis | • Structured enquiry<br>• determination of critical factors of success<br>• Balanced score card<br>• Evolution<br>• Current situation analysis |

**Table 3: procedures of information requirement determination**

According to Kcrmar (2005, p.62)

Within the mixed procedures the determination of critical factors of success as well as the balanced score card are most common. Therefore, they will be described more in detail and the remaining ones just briefly.

### 4.2.2.2.2 Subjective procedures

Open interview

In the open interview the respondent gets the task to characterize his information requirement. This will be supported be giving him example situations of his daily working environment, where the interviewee has the task to formulate questions.

Wish catalogue

The User of information will be presented a catalogue of possible information objects. Out of this, he has the task to choose those he thinks are necessary.

Enquiry of third

Here e.g. employees out of the near environment of the person, who is subject to the determination of information demand, or every third party, will be asked. This can be done by the procedures mentioned above and may lead to further information objects.

### 4.2.2.2.3 Objective procedures

Strategy analysis

Information requirement derives from the strategic objectives of the organisation or the management in the scope of strategic management.

Process analysis

It is used as instrument in the scope of models of the different levels of the organisation in the process of decision making. The information needed for the decision making processes refer to the information requirement of all participants of the process.

## Input-Process-Output analysis

This enlarges the process analysis. Information requirement and supply are treated as input and output ongoing with process steps.

## Decision analysis

It assumes that decision processes are structured and information requirement derives from every step of the decision making process.

### 4.2.2.2.4 Mixed procedures

## Structured enquiry

Questions for the interview derive from results of the process or strategic analysis. The questions may be commented or issues may be enlarged by the interviewee.

## Determination of critical factors of success

Critical factors of success are related to a close number of working sectors. Good results in these sectors are important to the organisation competing in the market.

This method is based upon the hypothesis that top management need information about the status of these critical factors of success. Therefore this method only copes with the information requirement of the top management level.

First of all it is necessary to formulate objectives. In a SME objectives of the organisation may are equal to the objectives of the management.

After that the critical factors have to be determined. Normally, they will be named out of the following resources (Rockart et al. 1981, pp. 14, cited in Schwarze 1998, pp.61):

- The branch in which the organisation operates has characteristic success factors
- Further success factors derive from the position which the organisation has in the branch

- Factors of the environment, which can be hardly influenced by the organisation, may create further success factors
- Temporary factors are critical in special situations which occur spontaneously in day to day business. Possibly, there could be an accident so that the delivery won't arrive in time. This creates the critical factor of the coordination of the logistic facilities, which only can be realised by the fast delivery of information to the correct recipient.

Those factors may be differentiated into internal and external ones. The determination may be achieved through an interview of the management by third, e.g. a consultancy. This has the advantage, that not only the internal view but also an external one will participate in the determination.

To secure that all relevant factors have been identified, the questions of the interview should be taken out of the resources and the answers afterwards should be compared with them.

The method of the determination of critical factors of success may and the derivative of the information requirement is also very favourable for the establishment of management information systems, which will be subject later.

Another advantage is that the determination is individual to each manager requirements.

The balanced scorecard (BSC)

This tool developed by Kaplan and Norton in the early 1990's (http://de.wikipedia.org/wiki/Balanced_Scorecard, 18.06.2006) enlarges the method of the determination of critical factors of success by involving not only the management in the determination but also all relevant stakeholders, which contribute to the main strategic aim of delivering value to the customer.

Its original purpose was the measurement of financial ratios not only with monetary data. They liked to involve Customers, Processes and Learning and development, also. Furthermore, the BSC was used as a tool of leading organisations.

The original BSC can be plot as follows:

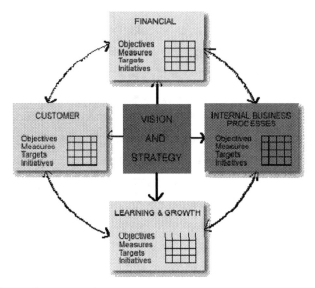

**Figure 4: balanced scorecard**

(http://www.marketingteacher.com/Lessons/lesson_balanced_scorecard.ht m, 18/06/2006)

The BSC, here, it is used to determine which information is needed by whom.

## 4.2.3 Communication requirement analysis

### 4.2.3.1 Key term and background

The analysis of communication requirement is the second main concern of the data flow analysis. Naturally, communication demand builds on the results of the information requirement analysis.

Communication derives from the Latin word "communicare" and means to inform somebody. It is the process of sending information to oneself or another entity. This process is alternately. Participants of communication are humans, animals and machines, e.g. data bases in a computer (http://en.wikipedia.org/wiki/Communication, 27/06/2006).

In general literature divides communication in horizontal and vertical communication. Former considers the communication between e.g. two persons at the same level, which is called complementary communication. Latter treats with the communication between two persons at different levels, e.g. between manager and secretary. This is called symmetric communication.

In the author's opinion, in business this differentiation is incorrect, because the term vertical leads to the assumption that e.g. an employee who wants to communicate with a colleague of his superior has to give this information to his superior first (vertical), who then transfers the information to his colleague (horizontal). By that, sometimes it is necessary to communicate diagonal. A communication model might be very individual to the organisations business.

Communication can adopt various forms. Those may be communication between machines, which can be digital. Furthermore, those can be communication between human beings, which can be verbal, non-verbal, visual, supported, in a paralanguage or with the help of gestures. Further forms are communication between a human and a machine, between individuals or groups, intimate or mass communication, telecommunication, chemical communication. Sometimes it is said, that unidirectional communication is communication, too. But concerning the original definition, where in communication at minimum one sender and one recipient are included, this is not a real form of communication (http://de.wikipedia.org/wiki/Kommunikation, 27/06/2006). This could be supported by the theological question: "If no-one heard the singing of a bird, has this singing really existed?" in connection with the aspect that communication in general leads to a reaction. The possibilities, here and especially in business, reach from ignoring the information given by the sender up to changing the whole strategy of the organisation caused by the meaning of the content of the information.

The concern of the communication requirement analysis is to deal with the origin of the information which than derives communication requirement and relations (Schwarze 1998, p. 107).

### 4.2.3.2    Methodology

Communication requirement analysis must specify communication partners, their connection, the media they use, time relation and the architecture of communication (Nettersheim, 2005, cited in Schwarze 1998, pp.63).

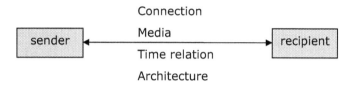

**Figure 5: communication process**

(own development)

Regarding to Schwarze (1998) these issues can be described as follows.

Communication partners in business have positions within or outside the organisation. Concerning latter, it is necessary to name the interfaces or ports used to get in contact with them.

Communication connections are whether direct or indirect. Direct communication describes a process where the communication partners are in direct contact, e.g. a conversation. The opposite is the using of a storage medium where information would get lost otherwise, e.g. a manager sends an e-mail because the person he wants to talk to, cannot be reached on phone or the information is too complex to provide it directly.

The relation to time deals with the delay of the arrival of the information at the recipient. If communication is simultaneously, the information will be delivered immediately e.g. in a telephone call, if not, it communication is retarded or delayed, e.g. by using the medium of a letter.

The architecture regards to the configuration and the possibilities of entry to the communication system. The system is closed, if only the communication partners have entry to it and third are closed out. This can be e.g. a private chat in the intranet. Otherwise, if third have entry to the system, it is open, e.g. telephone net.

The media of communication connect the communication partners. They can be classified by portable storage media, which can be analogue or digital, and pathways. A special medium for the transportation of information is air, which is used for direct face to face communication. Examples are:

**Table 4: examples of communication media**

| Media | | | | | |
|---|---|---|---|---|---|
| Portable storage | | Pathways | Air | | |
| analogue | Digital | | analogue | digital | |
| • Letter | • e-mail | • Fibre optic cable | • Direct con-versation | • Radio waves | |
| • Post card | • usb-stick | • Cupreous cable | • Smoke signs | • Funk signals to satellites and radio towers | |
| • notice | • compact disc | | | | |

Regarding to Schwarze (1998, pp. 64)

## 4.3 Concerns

### 4.3.1 Information quality

Information has to fulfil different requirements that it can be used in the most efficient way. Eppler (2003, p. 63) determines 70 criteria of information quality.

To keep practical lucidity the author will state the most important and systemize them afterwards.

#### 4.3.1.1 General criteria

Schwarze (1998, p. 94) determines less criteria of information quality, which seems to be the most important out of Epplers 70 criteria.

These are namely:

- Relevance   – Is the information helpful to fulfilling the task?
- Timeliness   – Is the information punctual or too late to fulfil the task?
- Actuality   – How old is the information?

- Reliability   – Is the information source and the information itself correct?
- Accuracy    – Is the information unambiguous and explicit?
- Completeness – Has the information the context required?
- Comprehensiveness – Is the information easy to understand?
- Applicability – Can the information used immediately to fulfil the task?
- Operating efficiency – Are costs and benefits in positive proportion?

The author evaluate this criteria as solid basis, but thinks it is important to add criteria of

- Objectivity
- Maintainability
- Appropriateness of meta-information

### 4.3.1.2    Criteria of information for management

Mintzberg (1980, cited in Schwarze 1998) states that information addressed to the management of an organisation has to meet leadership related concerns. Hence, management information must be presented in form which conforms the cognitive thinking of the manager. Mintzberg states more criteria, which conform to the general criteria as well and, therefore, will not be mentioned here again.

The author stresses the importance of actuality of information and that relevant information needs to be compressed, so that important decision can be made quickly.

### 4.3.1.3    Systemisation of information quality

According to Königer et al. (1998) all criteria of information quality can be systemised. To achieve this he tries to find appropriate headings or categories for all criteria, which relates to one dimension. A possible systemisation can be:

**Table 5: systemisation of information quality**

| Category | Dimension |
| --- | --- |
| Inner quality | Accuracy |
| | Objectivity |
| | Reliability |
| | Maintainability |
| Contextual quality | Relevance |
| | Completeness |
| | Applicability |
| | Appropriateness of meta-information |
| Time quality | Actuality |
| | Timeliness |
| Design quality | Comprehensiveness |
| | Factor of compression |

(according to Königer et al. (1998, p92.)

## 4.3.2 Information security

### 4.3.2.1    Background and aim

Information security is one of the most important concerns in the contemporary business environment.

Robbing internal information is interesting in the scope of industrial spying and attacks of hackers. Especially, intangible assets, e.g. software in development or concepts need to be protected. But also information about research and accountancy should not be accessible to the public or competitors.

Furthermore, data and information of customers must be protected to avoid misusing through third.

Therefore, several, measures to assure information security have to be taken.

### 4.3.2.2    Measures to protect information

According to Heinrich (2005, p.262) and Schwarze (1998, p.260) information can be protected on different levels:

#### 1. Level: Securing premises

This concerns the protecting of buildings, floors and rooms, where information is processed and stored. This can be achieved through entry controls and restrictions, respectively, permissions of access to information. Furthermore, non-electronically information can be stocked in lockable cabinets or saves.

#### 2. Level: Securing hardware

This concerns the protection of personal computers and portable storage media such as discs.

This can be achieved through bios passwords or copy and overwriting protection or internal firewalls and anti-spyware-software.

#### 3. Level: Securing network

As information is commonly exchanged in networks, the network itself must be protected. This can be realised through external firewalls as well as the construction of networks themselves. A wireless LAN network for example may be easier hacked as a cable network.

#### 4. Level: Securing software

The software where relevant information is processed must be secured, too. Here, the using of further passwords and access permissions, provided by the administrator is supposed, as well as the encryption of information.

## 5. Level: Security training for staff

As there is a high level of security, staff should be informed about these procedures and trained to use security measures in an appropriate way. The management should also allocate access permissions and stress the importance of information security and the responsibility connected to the grade of access permission.

## 4.3.3 Storage of information

Information can be stored in different ways. This may be electronically, namely, digital or in a physical, analogue way.

For some information the law dictates requirements to the storing of information, e.g. in Germany the storing of accountancy information, which must be realised over a period of time of 10 years in a medium which can be read all the time.

This aspect leads to the main concern of storing information, namely the ensuring that information can be read and processed over a long period of time.

One result of the exponential development of technology is the large variety of portable storage media. This large variety occurred because early media had insufficient storage capacity and it needed a relatively long time to write and read them. The users pushed to improvement.

By that, the first floppy-disc which had a size of 8 inch and a storing capacity of 180 KB (http://de.wikipedia.org/wiki/Diskette) transformed herself over a period of 20 years and several configurations to an USB-stick which has a size of a rubber and a current storing capacity of 8 GB, which is sold today. At the CEBIT a 16 GB version was presented, which will be released at second half of 2006. 8 BG is more than 46.000 times more than the capacity of the floppy-disc. USB Sticks with up to 64 GB are developed, but not sold until now (http://de.wikipedia.org/wiki/Usb-stick). The time needed to read and write these media shortened itself considerable, too.

Those transformations resulted in a large variety of hardware, which is necessary to read and write the media.

Another development was the compact disc and the DVD, which also has various configurations (CD: -R, -RW; DVD: DL, -R, +R, -RW, +RW) and storing capacity (CD: 700 – 800 MB; DVD: 4 - 8GB). The main concern here is the quality of the blank CD, because she determines the life time and, therefore, possible storage time of the information.

To connect all these facts leads to the following constraint:

*If information has to be stored over a long period of time, it is necessary to proof the quality of the storage media and to keep and to take care of the processing hardware.*

If the hardware gets lost, there will be no other possibility to read the information again.

To secure that information doesn't get lost following measures could be taken:

- Make regularly back up copies on different storage media
- Make back up copies on analogue media, if possible

The main advantage of analogue storage media is that it just can be destroyed by physical impacts, such as fire or water and that it will doesn't need complex processing hardware to get access to them.

But analogue storage media have also disadvantages. Information on analogue media can't in most cases processed or altered and it needs more time and expenses to transfer it.

## 4.4 Evaluation of the optimisation

There occur two major problems in the evaluation of costs and benefits. Firstly, the evaluation of the optimisation seems to be difficult, as there is no real possibility to assign any amount of money to the success of it.

Secondly, an optimisation of data flow takes also effect on the long term and cost of it may occur just on the short term, which also makes it difficult to relate benefits and costs.

To evaluate benefits the author identified the value-benefit-analysis as a tool which can be adapted. Horváth (1996, p.505) criticises this instrument as insufficient and recommends to execute an investment appraisal every time. But this must be seen under critical determination of the size and the content of the project. It is obviously, that the decision to build a house by the use of option A may have more value-benefit than under option B and that these options must be valued also under monetary criteria. But in a decision, that secretary A sits in future between secretary B and C (in the past B she sat in middle) to achieve more efficient communication, an investment appraisal seems practically disproportionate.

The value-benefit-analysis is a multidimensional analysis used originally to evaluate action alternatives in the decision making process, which are not comparable in a monetary way. Heinrich (2005, pp.379) adapted this analysis to evaluate alternatives in IT-projects.

The main advantage of this analysis is that it relates several criteria, which are difficult to compare among each other, to their contribution to the achievement of the overall aim. Further advantages are that alternatives are comparable directly and that the analysis offers a lot of flexibility (http://de.wikipedia.org/wiki/Nutzwertanalyse). A disadvantage is that the criteria often are evaluated from a very subjective view.

To execute a value-benefit-analysis the following preconditions must be fulfilled

Firstly, all alternatives are concerning the problem. Likewise, the preferences of the alternatives have to be complete. An existence of an preference "P" must be fulfilled, which means that all alternatives can be related among each other (A is better or equal or worse than B [this is mathematically expressed trough: P(A,B)]). These relations must also be transitive, which means that if option A is better than option C and C is worse than option B, A has to be better than or equal to C.

The mathematical expression of the value-benefits-analysis is a function "u" and is expressed trough the following term:

$$(u(A)>u(B)) \leftrightarrow P\ (A,B)$$

The alternatives "x" have different criteria "k", which can be weighted of their importance through "g". The sum of "g" of each alternative equal 1 or 100%:

$$\sum_{i=1}^{n} = g_i = 1$$

Every alternative has different criteria "y", where "n" is the number of these criteria and "i" is the running index for the criteria and "j" the running index for the alternatives. This leads to the complete value-benefit formula:

$$u(x_j) = \sum_{i=1}^{n} g_i \times u(y_i)$$

Some criteria may that important, that their fulfilment decides whether to use an alternative or not. Such a criterion is named KO-criterion.

It is important to state, that "u" has no dimension. This means if u(A)=2 and u(B)=1, option A is not double worth than B. The difference between both gives only an idea if one alternative is just a little bit better than the other or it is absolutely better than the other one.

According to Zangemeister (1976, cited in Heinrich et al. 2005, pp. 380) the value-benefit analysis of an optimisation of data flow consists of six important steps.

First of all, the main aim has to be identified, which is the "what is to need to know" or relating to figure 3 it is information number 5.

This information can be communicated in different ways with the help of different media, which are the alternatives, which have to be identified in the second step. These alternatives should also contain the current communication, to make it comparable with the proposed one.

In the third step the criteria have to be identified, which derive from the tasks of the management of information economies (right time, right place, right quality etc.).

Now, these criteria must be weighted and if necessary clarified as a KO-criterion.

After that the value-benefit of each criterion must be determined. According to Heinrich et al. (2005, p.382) this can be realised by a using different scales. The first one is the nominal scale, e.g. "criteria fulfilled" or "criteria not fulfilled", which is very superficial. The second one is the ordinal scale, e.g. the system of school marks, and finally, the cardinal scale, which is related to measurable items (e.g. weight or time). Here, in this case the author proposes to use an ordinal scale (0: absolutely not fulfilled up to 5: absolutely fulfilled) to differentiate the nominal scale deeper.

The last step then is to calculate the overall value-benefit from all alternatives and to make a decision.

The matrix for the example of the information of the delivery order of the chain store to the stock would look as follows:

**Table 6: benefit matrix**

| Target information: | | Delivery order | |
|---|---|---|---|
| criteria | Importance | Current media (e.g. telephone) | Possible media (e.g. fax) |
| **Right time** (in time, immediately) | 0,4 | 5 | 5 |
| **Right quality** | 0,1 | 4 | 5 |
| **Right address** (stock, office, accounting) | 0,3 | 3 | 5 |
| **Right form** (written[paper, electronic]oral) | 0,2 | 1 | 5 |
| Σ | 1 | **3,5** | **5** |

(own development)

It is obvious, that an order by a fax form would be more favourable than an order by phone.

The decision is dependent on the value benefit and the costs of implementing the alternative.

Former, may be executed by using the rule of majority, which is common utilized in the case of exercising an ordinal scale (Heinrich et al. 2005, p.

384). This rule says that the alternative which is in most cases better than the other alternatives is favoured for an implementation.

Thus the value-benefit has no dimension it is wrong to relate costs directly to it, which is the latter factor for decision making.

Literature does not give any theoretical answer to this problem. By that the author suggests a practical solution. Namely, to evaluate critically with the commonsense (as it is often in practice the case), if an investment in the implementation of the result of the analysis will be balanced to its costs.

There, not only direct costs of e.g. the installation of a certain electronic system, but also the time invested and the trouble in processes caused while implementation should be taken into account.

This all together, should be also set against the organisations size and financial health.

To get a more objective view, the decision making process should be executed in a so called problem saving group, which could contain of the top management as well as line managers and a third party, e.g. a consultancy.

## 4.5 Management Information systems (MIS)

David Kroenke et al. (1994) provides the most practice orientated view of MIS. Although his work is from the year 1994, his explanations are applicable, because he stresses more the organisational than the technical side. Therefore, his work written in co-operation with Richard Hatch will be the basis for the following explanations.

### 4.5.1 Definition and background

Firstly, a system is a unit of interrelated components, which are working in a certain way together (Microsoft Encarta 2006).Systems may be open or closed. If a system interacts with its environment it is open (Kroenke et al. 1994, p.21).

An information system processes input into output. In addition, they consist of three elements: the people, the procedures and the data. If a MIS is supported by computers the information system has further two elements, namely the hard- and the software.

The relationship between the components of a computer aided MIS is expressed best by the following figure:

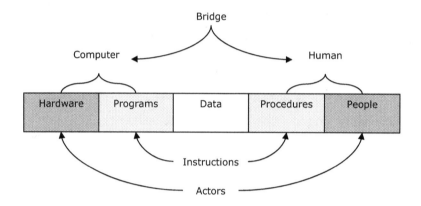

**Figure 6: Relationship among components of MIS**

(Kroenke et al. 1994, p.24)

Kroenke (1994, p. 6) states that the term of management information systems may be misleading, because according to Keen (1980, cited in Kroenke 1994, p.6) a MIS is "the effective design, delivery and use of information systems in organisations". Obviously, this definition does not contain the term of management.

Thus, the definition of MIS is broader than the term itself does imply.

The subject of MIS does not only cover the informational management in the scope of managers. Furthermore, it draws itself through the whole organisation. All members must be involved.

But as the effective design, delivery and use of information systems seems to be part of the management of information economies, the definition regarding to Kroenke (1994, p.6) needs to be adjusted to:

*"MIS is the development and effective use of information systems in organisations."*

## 4.5.2 Tasks

First of all, it is important to state that not the organisation uses information, people do. Hence, the most important task of a MIS is to be handle able by humans.

Another overall task is to coordinate departments that the organisation is able to respond as a unit. Therefore, the technology used is less important than having the appropriate information flow on a timely basis (Kroenke et al. 1994, p.5).

A further task is to support all personnel within their functions. This means not only to provide the required information, but also to support them within the management process (planning organizing, implementing, controlling).

## 4.5.3 Operating on different levels

### 4.5.3.1    The need for different levels

Scientists examine different levels in business administration. The number of levels is dependent upon the general organisation of the company. A SME, as example, would have 3 levels. The first level is the individual, topped by the work group or departmental level and this again topped from the enterprise level. If this small enterprise would be bought by a large group, another level would top the other three. By that the architecture of a MIS will also be based upon those levels. For the further examination an SME approach will be described, according to the tasks and element defined by Kroenke et al. (1994).

### 4.5.3.2    The levels of a MIS

#### 4.5.3.2.1    The personal information system (PIS)

According to Kroenke (1994, pp.169) the first level has three important tasks to solve. Firstly, it has to guarantee interpersonal communication. This contains not only the mailing or word processing, but also the desk top publishing and presentation software, by that an individual is able to catch up most important information and present it in a compressed and stylish way.

The second task of PIS is to act as a system for analysis. Subjects may reach from data of sales related to customers up to the analysis of schedules. Likewise, the PIS needs to have access to external data and should be able to process analysed data in a statistical way.

The third task is to provide tasks of tracking and monitoring, which involves database and project management applications.

An actual requirement of PIS is that all components are able to communicate among each other and data is compatible. Such a totally integrated system provides Microsoft® with its Office® application. But as this is programmed in a careless way (produces lots of errors and it is sometimes insufficient to the users requirements) and is cost intensive for users, first cost free applications are on the market, e.g. OpenOffice.org®. These application fights also against the Microsoft's monopoly.

The values added by PIS are the facilitation of personal processes and the initiating of change, which is survival decisive in today's business environment, and the advancement of personal products.


### 4.5.3.2.2  The work group information system (WIS)

According to Kroenke (1994, pp. 333) a workgroup is differentiated in two ways. Firstly, it always consists of different people. If all members fulfil the nearly same task, the workgroup is homogeneous, e.g. accounting invoices. Otherwise, the workgroup is heterogeneous, e.g. a project team. Additionally, workgroups may co-operate temporarily, e.g. project work groups, or permanent, e.g. the marketing department.

In general it is to say, that WIS consists of connected PIS. They share different components to achieve a common goal or to fulfil a common task. Within PIS not only hardware (e.g. a printer) but also information via a local area network (LAN) is shared. This LAN facilitates communication, make group conferences possible. Moreover, concerning e.g. a project, PIS make it possible to put together individual parts to a major project, which is named collaborative working. Furthermore, it provides service for group decision making by providing a workgroup shared database.

Another task of WIS is to coordinate workgroup schedule, by coordinating appointments of each member.

The values added by WIS are in general the same as in the PIS, but they go deeper. This is achieved through the facilitation of resource allocation and strategic management (e.g. decision making and planning within the group). In relation to the facilitation of change this means also, that it is possible to involve a large variety of opinions and ideas to push innovation and improvement.

### 4.5.3.2.3   The organisational information system (OIS)

On the organisational level, there are several sub stages, which are divided into their contribution to the potential benefit in relation to their degree of business transformation. This analysis was established by the MIT's Loan School of Management (cited in Kroenke et al. 1994, pp. 518) and 12 major enterprises.

The stages can be plotted as follows:

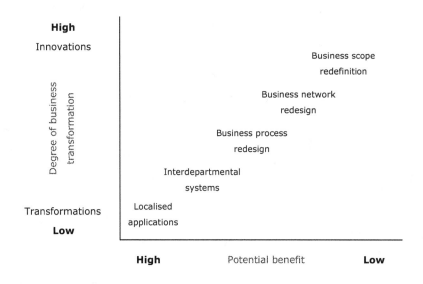

**Figure 7: Categories of OIS**

(Kroenke et al. 1994, p.519)

The first level contains the localised applications, which are the PIS and WIS. The second stage extends WIS by providing integrated information support to all departments of the organisation. On the next level, an information system would integrate all departments in processes of e.g. the development of a product line.

Business network redesign establishes interfaces with organisations outside the organisation. Here, employees might enter directly orders into the suppliers' information system or knowledge networks are established.

The last stage is business scope redefinition enables the company to create fundamental changes in its products and services which it provides. An example for this last stage is DELL, which has achieved the so called virtual integration of the supply chain and set standards in the new economy business that its competitors did not achieved until today.

The values added through OIS are established on the same stages, namely, process, product and change. But in difference to PIS and WIS these values are applied more on the strategic level.

## 4.5.4 Further parts of a MIS

Kroenke et al. (1994, pp. 687) suggests the incorporation of two further systems into the MIS. These are Decision Support Systems and Knowledge Systems.

### 4.5.4.1    Decision Support Systems (DSS)

A DSS draws itself trough all organisational levels and facilitates the solution of unstructured problems. Consequently, they facilitate the decision making process. Hence, DSS are used by personnel which has to decide something and the DSS must be adjusted to the decisions they have to make.

A DSS is a flexible system which can consist of different tools and models, which may be employed individually.

With the help of a DSS the user is able to apply a large variety of data into individual developed models that than are able to create scenarios.

The main functions of DSS are to identifying trends, predict decision outcomes, compute optimum mixes, facilitate in general, to determine sensitive variables and to act as catalyst for change.

Finally it is important to state, that a DSS must be programmed as individual as the MIS itself.

### 4.5.4.2    Knowledge Systems (KS)

Knowledge Systems are interrelated with concerns of strategic human resource development. The University of Sunderland (2004, pp. 289) identified knowledge system as a trend of e-learning.

The main tasks of these systems are to make training more individual, to reduce time and cost of training and to connect knowledge and to save it centrally. A public knowledge system is wikipedia.org, where authors all over the world are able to add articles. The only problem of wikipedia.org is that sometimes the control of the editorial office is that overtaxed that added information is not proofed quickly enough.

Knowledge systems differ in the interaction. As the levels by Kroenke et al. seem to be out of date, the author developed a systemisation on her own, containing the following levels:

The first stage is the static availability of documents, which can be read. The next stage, which can be seen as the first stage of training, is the integration of multiple choice tests to proof if the relevant information has been caught. The following stage does this in a more interactive way containing multimedia applications. The next then step is to integrate a virtual campus where people, independently from location and time zone, may change ideas. And the last level is the integration of group projects within this campus.

A future development of multimedia applications could be that the software acts individually in the training process to the members' requirements and peaks a real dialogue with them. The target key term for that is artificial intelligence.

# 5 A optimisation of data flow for art decor®

## 5.1 History and business of the organisation

art décor® GmbH is a medium sized enterprise located in Bad Köstritz(Germany). It was founded in 1998 and is today a medium sized retailer with four chain stores. These stores are situated in Zwickau, Gera and Leipzig in Shopping malls, because retailing has explored its concentration there. The stores have an average size of 300 m². Additionally art decor(r)(r) sells its goods at mall events on Easter, Christmas and other possibilities as they arise.

art decor® trades with a large variety of gifts and decoration articles. Their portfolio is a mixture of high quality brand articles like Leonardo® glass, Dreamlight® or Sheepworld® as well as high quality imports from China.

CEOs of art decor® are Mr. Lockschen and Mr. Oppel. In the main office in Bad Köstritz, furthermore, are working Mr. Kürbs as Sales Manager, Ms. Schönfeld as accountant and Mr. Mollek in the operative service. The author is also employed under a self employed agreement as mall event coordinator. In the whole art decor® employs 24 staff members.

In the last year art decor® generated a turn-over of 3 million Euros. The business gets more and more seasonal and the highest sales volume is generated before holidays.

As retailing business gets more and more complicated, art decor® started to explore its competitive advantage by covering the niche of high quality interim solutions. The two main mall operators ECE and MFI follow the policy that a store in their mall is rented over 10 years and longer. This seems to be connected with a certain risk in times of stagnation in the German economy. By that, malls often have a problem to find a new lessee. As art decor® started in Gera with the opening of their shop with a preparation time of two weeks, they got known for their high quality flexibility. Over time, they developed and improved a store equipment system, which allows them to open up a perfect looking shop within two to four weeks. Now, malls often rent a shop to art decor® for an uncertain amount of time (differ from 3 moths to one year) until they have found a lessee who is willing to sign a 10 year contact. By that, malls are happy that they have no empty shops and art decor® reduces its overall risk. A further result of this policy is an often changing amount in shops and employees.

As storage space is not shop space and, by that, is a cost factor, goods have to be allocated carefully, which requires well developed communication policies.

## 5.2 Data Flow analysis

### 5.2.1 Preface concerning methodology

The author had the intention to use a questionnaire for the analysis. The especially developed questionnaire contained a mix of information and communication requirement analysis as well as a subtle evaluation of information processes. Therefore, the author developed a special system of colours to determine deficits, satisfaction and needs. Also the weighting is contained (please see appendix 1 and 2). As the weighting in the questionnaire is based on school marks the author would have transformed the results into the original system.

The CEO of art decor® considered the questionnaire as too complicated for his staff. By that, the author changed her strategy and developed in co-operation with the CEO an open interview, containing themes of order, delivery, responsibility, accounting and personnel. This open interview structure where then executed in a collective meeting in the office and with each chain store manager.

The following part exposures deficits of the information flow as well as the main concerns.

## 5.2.2 Analysis and recommendations

### 5.2.2.1    Organisation and communication structure

In general it is to say that art decor® communicates in a very simple way, the usage of high technology is avoided by its liability of breakdown, hindering to change locations and staff quickly. The adaptation time for a new interim store would last too long.

Most used and also most preferred communication media by all members of the organisation are telephone and fax.

As the organisation structure is kept very simple, the communication structure seems to be more complex:

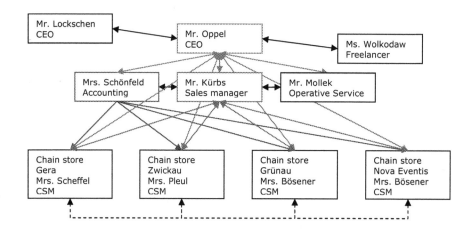

**Figure 8: Communication structure**

(own development)

Firstly, Mr. Oppel is communicating with every part of his company. This gives him insight in all processes and concerns. Sometimes this leads to an information overload especially in time before Christmas. Additionally, this system may also have its limitations. As art decor® consisted of 6 stores sometimes information got lost or was delivered too late. This in connection with the Christmas business and the Christmas mall sales was felt by the employees as to much for Mr Oppel.

Secondly, this structure also makes it necessary, that all members know who to ask if they have problems and to whom they have to deliver their information. This causes fewer problems because the office is just one room and the chain store managers also know whom to contact.

Furthermore, this structure shows, that Mrs. Schönfeld communicates more in a one way manner, because in general the chain store mangers have no questions to her. All bills are firstly authorised by Mr. Oppel, before they are paid.

As the dashed arrows suggest it, the communication between the chain stores is rudimentary. They only call each other to ask for goods, which are off stock in their own store and demanded by a customer immediately. The management started to organise a chain store management meeting twice a year, where also experiences and actual development are exchanged. One chain store manager wished to widen this communication, by e.g. getting turn over figures of the other stores, which she than wishes to use as motivation tool for staff.

## 5.2.2.2    The main office

The analysis showed to major problems in the office. Firstly, nobody does exactly know when a colleague is in the office or at an exhibition or for shopping in China or on holidays.

By that the author supposes to install a large white calendar, where every exhibition and other events are marked. Every colleague gets his own colour; these colours are now used to mark who takes part in the exhibition or who is in China. Also these colours are used to sign every members holiday period.

Regarding to the colours used in the communication structure an example, where Mr. Oppel and Mr. Kürbs are visiting an exhibition on different dates, could look as follows:

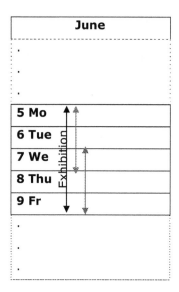

**Figure 9: Example new calendar**

(own development)

Birthdays of all staff should be also plotted there, because it leads to better corporate climate, if Mrs. Schönfeld is able to congratulate staff.

Furthermore, Mrs. Schönfeld likes to know the appointments of Mr. Kürbs as well as those of Mr. Oppel, to be able to estimate when they are back in office and if it is possible to call them on their mobile. This information could be incorporated in the Monday's meeting, where general tasks and problems of the week are discussed.

The second main problem is, that in the office shift plans of the chain stores are hidden in archives. This leads to the problem that the office tries to reach staff in the stores which is absent and, therefore, stresses chain store staff by storing and delivering information for their colleagues. Especially in Christmas time staff feels disturbed by that and they feel that their writing of shift plans is wastage of time, because in Bad Köstritz nobody reads them.

By that the author suggests to install a magnetic board, which is a blank form of shifts and staff are the magnets in the office, where shift plans have to be plotted by e.g. Mrs. Schönfeld directly after the incoming of them.

A further suggestion of the author is to analyse deeper the figures of turnover. Actually, the daily turnover figures of each store are compared with the daily figures of the year before, by integrating them in the form. But a general overview over larger periods is not produced. If this would be done, it would be easier to identify trends in turn over and the management could react better on that.

In conclusion, the information in the office is stored orderly (although it doesn't seem so at the first view) in archives that every body knows where to look for the information required.

### 5.2.2.3    Chain stores

As each chain store has the same task, the required information seems to be equal, but often the daily business and the individuality of the chain store manager developed different solutions for these concerns.

<u>Similarities</u>

A common point of dissatisfaction is the current system of delivery. The order delivery works at the moment in following scheme:

Chain stores order their goods in two different ways. At the one side they place their order directly at the sales agents of the different suppliers. If it is not possible to place direct their order, they order it informal from Bad Köstritz. Therefore, they receive deliveries of the stock of Bad Köstritz as well as from the suppliers.

The stores don't receive any information of the date and time of delivery of the suppliers. In the past this was so, but without any reason it is not provided by them anymore. They also don't receive information from Bad Köstritz when they receive their delivery from stock and what this delivery contains. Sometimes Mr. Oppel or Mr. Kürbs calls from on the way, sometimes they don't.

All chain store managers wished to receive information at least one day before delivery, that they receive delivery and what the delivery contains to coordinate this with external deliveries. They don't see any necessity in regular deliveries.

Regarding the content they assess it as more important to know, which sort of goods are inside than the quantity of goods delivered. By that they feel able to adjust their next order, because until the whole delivery is sighted Mr. Oppel or Mr. Kürbs want to take the next order with them. Sometimes Mr Kürbs places an order himself when he visits the store. This, the chain managers think worse the effect that orders often are doubled and goods have to be send back to stock.

Besides that, it is sometimes the case that the chain store managers order goods at the sales agents, which were ordered some time ago at an exhibition. By that orders are also doubled placed and so much the worse that there are now different prices for the same good, which leads to difficulties in the accountancy.

Furthermore, they would like to know, if the delivery doesn't contain a customers order, why this is so, because if the ordered good is not available anymore they would like to tell this customer as soon as possible.

Additionally, by an early call they would have the possibility to communicate which goods are not needed.

The main office develops at the moment a general catalogue, where all goods are listed and can be ordered with the help of bar codes and the cash system. This catalogue is also wished by all chain store managers.

By the developing of this catalogue and, therefore, the adjusting of the order and delivery system, the author advises art decor® urgently to integrate the aspects mentioned above.

A further point of lack of information is the holiday planning or absence planning of staff from the office in Bad Köstritz. By that, chain store mangers would be able to save time and costs, because they would not e.g. try to reach Mr Oppel the whole day to get to know at the end, that he is in China and that they must speak to Mr. Kürbs now. This plan could be provided in a form of a monthly calendar which then is placed in the back offices of the stores.

Another lack of information occurs in the case of reclamations. These are placed in general at the sales agents, who then give feedback to Bad Köstritz, but the main office then doesn't give that feedback to the stores again.

Concerning data security, the author has identified a lack of securing the data relevant to accountancy. The so called Z-Bons, which is the daily accounting of the cash system, are stored orderly in an archive, but are not stocked in a locked or fire protected way.

If customers order goods, which are not available in store, they leave only their name and their number. This information is cancelled after usage.

Here the author proposes to store this information and to send use the addresses to get to know more about customers and to establish a customer relationship, e.g. by sending incentives at their birthdays.

All the other data is stored orderly in archives.

<u>Differences</u>

The first point for improvement sees the author in the information delivery between the shifts. The chain store manager e.g. in Zwickau provides important information for the next shift in the one hour of overlapping of the shifts. In contrast in Gera and in Leipzig information is collected on little sheets which are placed next to the cash system. Here the author advises the use of a little book, which is placed next to the cash system, too. In this book, all information could be noted in. By that the danger of getting lost of notes would be minimised and past processes and circumstances would be easier controllable.

In Zwickau the chain store manager has improved the system of storing the information from the centre management, Bad Köstritz and suppliers. She has introduced a little book, where each case is noted regarding its incoming and work off. This system should be adapted by the other stores to make processes better controllable. Furthermore, if a good is not available and must be ordered from a sales agent, the note with the customers name and address the sales person sticks it at the list of the sales agent. This could also be adapted by the other stores.

## 5.2.2.4    Stock and inventory

At the moment information of stock can be hardly provided only by physical counting. By that, sometimes goods fall into oblivion.

In the author's opinion, this is a major starting point for improvement. At the moment there is no possibility to calculate a stock conversion cycle and use this then as a control tool. Furthermore, questions concerning stock need too much time to answer.

The interview with the CEO Mr. Oppel showed that art decor® has started to rearrange its whole stock, order and delivery system, which also contains a special integrated cash system in the stores. But at the moment art decor® is in the early research and development phase, where the requirements on this system are collected and information is too vague to present it here. art decor® plans with the final introduction of this system in 2 or 3 years.

One important factor concerning this system, that art decor® has identified, is that the order system should not be too automated. As their business is season and taste dependent, the common sense of a human being can adjust order quantities better than a computer could do it ever.


## 5.2.2.5    Sales at mall events

The information flow concerning the organisation of special mall sales in general has no deficits, as the author and the CEO every time send mail copies among each other. By that, everybody knows which information the centre managers got.

The only problem which the author identifies is an information lack which leads to a hinder in decision making, as she has always to ask for feedback, before she is able to accept orally a renting space in a mall. As some managers realised this, they started to call Mr. Oppel directly. By that, the author wishes information about the period, the duration, the size and maximum costs of each mall sale.

At the moment the portfolio of the mall sales is adjusted by Mr. Oppel, where the author has the possibility to contribute with her ideas. After this adjusting, a detailed range of goods which are available to present in the mall, is wished by the author, too.

### 5.2.3 Implementing a MIS?

The implementation of a management information system at art decor® seems to be difficult, because of the light and reasonable aversion of information technical equipment. In the office there is one PC, used by all. Hence, art decor® should try to implement an analogue system. Which firstly contains of the mentioned above calendar (WIS), shift and turn over plan (OIS). By that, daily and fresh information is plotted on the walls.
A suggestion of the author concerning also the new stock management system looks as follows:

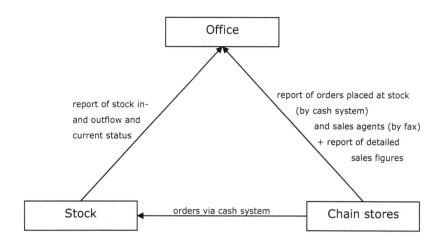

**Figure 10: a stock related MIS**
(own development)

To implement such as system, it is necessary to gather each article and to gather all information of the article. This leads to a high administrative expense. Concerning the changing portfolio of products the author suggests to hire further staff and hardware to fill the data base quickly with information the first time. Adjusting the data after its initiation needs to and will cause less administrative expense.

In Conclusion it is to say, that the implementation of a high technology MIS, which is required in these and future days, in a short period of time won't make any sense. The author, thinks that art decor® could have created a future competitive advantage by staying analogue in the digital age.

# 6  Conclusion

This work has shown, that the management of information and data flow in theory and practice are fairly different, and that theoretical techniques sometimes may not be applicable in practice.

The author was amazed how varied these topics are treated in literature and how many technical rather than practical views are presented there. She further noted that literature cites itself completely very often and just names the topic in a different way.

The analysis of art decor ® showed that in practice the management of data flow and the analysis itself are highly dependent to the people employed in such an organisation. Furthermore the analysis has shown, that the assumption of the introduction, that sometimes an objective improvement is not applicable of subjective reasons, is true and that this sometimes evaluated by common sense is correct.

The author regrets that the time at the end was not sufficient to implement the suggestions identified in the analysis and to evaluate the success of the optimisation.

# 7 Appendices

## Appendix 1: Users manual questionnaire

Hallo liebe(r) Mitarbeiter/in,

Mein Name ist Anne Wolkodaw, und normaler Weise bin ich bei art decor(r) für die Organisation der Sonderstände zuständig und führe Promotionaktionen durch.

### Worum geht's?

Heute wende ich mich im Rahmen meiner Diplomarbeit (die ich am 21.7.07 abgeben muss) an Sie, in der ich es mir zum Ziel gemacht ein Konzept zur Verbesserung der Kommunikation in der Firma zu erarbeiten. Es geht darum heraus zu finden, welche Information, wann, wie und wo gebraucht wird, damit Sie Ihre Arbeit so gut wie möglich erledigen können.

Da es dabei also um Sie und Ihre tägliche Arbeit geht, erhalten Sie mit dem folgenden Fragebogen die Möglichkeit, diese aktiv mitzugestalten.

### Wie funktioniert der Bogen?

Das Thema ist sehr komplex, was auch den Bogen sehr komplex macht, aber ich habe Ihn versucht so einfach wie möglich zu gestalten.

Damit aber nichts schief geht, nehmen Sie den Bogen bitte mit nach Hause und füllen Ihn dort in Ruhe aus. Des Weiteren, habe ich unten zu jedem Schritt ein Beispiel aufgeführt, und damit Sie den Überblick nicht verlieren, können sie ruhig die Anleitung neben den Bogen legen(Bitte lesen Sie die Anleitung komplett bevor Sie anfangen).

1. Bitte füllen Sie den Kopf des Bogens aus.

   Beispiel:

   > *Position: Filialleiterin*
   >
   > *Ort: Filiale Zwickau*

2. Bitte suchen Sie sich drei unterschiedlich farbige Stifte (z.B. blau, rot und grün) und malen sie mit je einer Farbe die Kästchen vor „Soll", „Ist" und „Neutral" aus.

   Beispiel:

   ▨ *Soll(grün)*

   ▨ *Ist (rot)*

   ▨ *Neutral(blau)*

   Was bedeutet das:

   > *Bsp.: Die Information, dass eine Warenlieferung kommt, wurde Ihnen per Telefon mitgeteilt. Das gefällt Ihnen so nicht, dann schreiben Sie bitte „Telefon" in ▨ (rot) und da Sie diese Information viel lieber per Mail hätten, schreiben Sie „Mail" in derselben Zeile in ▨ (grün). Sollte aber alles ok sein, dass heißt Sie bekommen die Info per Mail wie Sie es gerne hätten, dann schreiben Sie bitte „Mail" in ▨ (blau).*

   **Wichtig: Diese Farbkodierung ist nur für 2. Teil im Fragebogen notwendig!**

3. Füllen Sie nun den Teil zum Informationsbedarf aus.

In 2.1 können Sie Aussagen darüber machen, welche Informationen (z.B. bezüglich Sortiment, Lieferungen, Personal, Abrechnung, etc.) Sie im alltäglichen Geschäftsleben brauchen, und wie und von wem Sie diese bekommen/bekommen müssen und wie wichtig einzelne Kriterien sind. Um das auszudrücken hilft wieder die Farbkodierung weiter. Die Wichtigkeit bewerten Sie bitte mit Schulnoten (bitte vergeben Sie dabei jede Note möglichst nur einmal).

Beispiel 1:

| Infor-mation | Von wem? | Medium | Qualität der Information bezüglich | | | Wie ge-speichert? |
|---|---|---|---|---|---|---|
| | | | Zeit | Kontext | Form | |
| Waren-liefer-ung (blau) | Aus-hilfe(rot) Herr Kürbs (grün) | Mündlich auf dem Weg zum Klo (rot) E-Mail (grün) | ☐ Pünktlich (Termin:...... ............) ☒ Sofort (blau) ☐..................... ............ | ☒ Vollständig (grün) ☐ verständlich ☐ objektiv ☐ ..................... | ☒ Ordentlich zusammen-gefasst ☐..................... ................ | ☒ Gar nicht ☐ Abgeordnet ☐ Im PC gespeichert ☐ .................. ............ |
| | 5 | 4 | 1 | 2 | 3 | 6 |

Bedeutung:

*Die Aushilfe teilt Ihnen in der Regel auf dem Weg zum Klo mit, dass sie gerade eben erfahren hat, dass Morgen eine Warenlieferung kommt. Leider hat sie vergessen zu erwähnen, dass sie eventuell fehlende Waren noch nachmelden sollen. Ihnen ist es eigentlich egal, wer Ihnen diese Information mitteilt, Hauptsache, sie kommt pünktlich, vollständig und geordnet.*

Beispiel 2:

| Infor-mation | Von wem? | Medium | Qualität der Information bezüglich | | | Wie ge-speichert? |
|---|---|---|---|---|---|---|
| | | | Zeit | Kontext | Form | |
| Urlaubs-planung in Bad Köstritz (grün) | Herr Kürbs (grün) | E-Mail (grün) | ☒ Pünktlich (grün) (Termin:...... ............) ☐ Sofort (blau) ☐ ..................... ............ | ☒ Vollständig (grün) ☐ verständlich ☐ objektiv ☐ ..................... | ☒ Ordentlich zusammen-gefasst (grün) ☐..................... ................... | ☐ Gar nicht ☐ Abgeordnet ☐ Im PC gespeichert ☒ Aushang (grün) |
| | 5 | 4 | 1 | 2 | 3 | 3 |

Bedeutung:

*Sie wünschen Sich, dass Sie pünktlich über die Urlaubsplanung in der Hauptverwaltung informiert zu werden, damit Sie z. B. Herrn Oppel nicht mit weniger wichtigen Problemen im Urlaub belästigen. Damit auch alle anderen in der Filiale Bescheid wissen, möchten sie diese Planung im Umkleideraum aufhängen. Bis jetzt ist das aber ist das aber so nie geschehen.*

Bei Informationen, die Sie kriegen, aber nicht haben wollen, weil Sie irrelevant sind, tragen Sie diese bitte einfach unter 2.2 ein.

4. Füllen Sie bitte nun den Teil zur Informationssicherheit aus. Hier können Sie einfach ankreuzen und/oder Ihre Antwort aufschreiben. Die Farbe ist dabei unwichtig.

Ja und das ist eigentlich auch schon alles. Wenn Sie Fragen zum Ausfüllen haben, oder nicht so recht wissen was sie schreiben sollen können sie mich gerne unter: 0179/768414 anrufen. Ich rufe Sie dann umgehend zurück und helfe Ihnen gerne.

Ich möchte mich an dieser Stelle schon einmal ganz herzlich bedanken, dass Sie mir helfen und sich die Zeit nehmen und die Mühe machen, den Bogen auszufüllen und ihn <u>bis spätestens Montag Vormittag nach Bad Köstritz abschicken</u>. Die entstandenen Kosten für Porto ersetzte ich Ihnen selbstverständlich gerne. Vielen Dank!!!!

# Appendix 2: Questionnaire

## 1. Allgemeine Angaben

Position:

☐ Soll     ☐ Ist     Ort/Filiale:     ☐ Neutral

## 2. Informationsbedarf

### 2.1

| Information (Aussage/Bedeutung) | Von wem? | Benutztes Medium (Fax, Telefon etc.) | Qualität der Information bezüglich | | | Wie gespeichert? |
|---|---|---|---|---|---|---|
| | | | Zeit | Kontext | Form | |
| | | | ☐ Pünktlich (Termin:............) ☐ Sofort ☐ | ☐ vollständig ☐ verständlich ☐ objektiv ☐ | ☐ Ordentlich zusammengefasst ☐ | ☐ Gar nicht ☐ Abgeordnet ☐ Im PC gespeichert ☐ |
| | | | ☐ Pünktlich (Termin:............) ☐ Sofort ☐ | ☐ vollständig ☐ verständlich ☐ objektiv ☐ | ☐ Ordentlich zusammengefasst ☐ | ☐ Gar nicht ☐ Abgeordnet ☐ Im PC gespeichert ☐ |
| | | | ☐ Pünktlich (Termin:............) ☐ Sofort ☐ | ☐ vollständig ☐ verständlich ☐ objektiv ☐ | ☐ Ordentlich zusammengefasst ☐ | ☐ Gar nicht ☐ Abgeordnet ☐ Im PC gespeichert ☐ |
| | | | ☐ Pünktlich (Termin:............) ☐ Sofort ☐ | ☐ vollständig ☐ verständlich ☐ objektiv ☐ | ☐ Ordentlich zusammengefasst ☐ | ☐ Gar nicht ☐ Abgeordnet ☐ Im PC gespeichert ☐ |

| Information (Aussage/Bedeutung) | Von wem? | Benutztes Medium(Fax, Tel etc.) | Qualität der Information bezüglich | | | Wie gespeichert? |
|---|---|---|---|---|---|---|
| | | | Zeit | Kontext | Form | |
| | | | □ Pünktlich (Termin:.........) □ Sofort □ | □ vollständig □ verständlich □ objektiv □ | □ Ordentlich zusammengefasst □ | □ Gar nicht □ Abgeordnet □ Im PC gespeichert □ |
| | | | □ Pünktlich (Termin:.........) □ Sofort □ | □ vollständig □ verständlich □ objektiv □ | □ Ordentlich zusammengefasst □ | □ Gar nicht □ Abgeordnet □ Im PC gespeichert □ |
| | | | □ Pünktlich (Termin:.........) □ Sofort □ | □ vollständig □ verständlich □ objektiv □ | □ Ordentlich zusammengefasst □ | □ Gar nicht □ Abgeordnet □ Im PC gespeichert □ |
| | | | □ Pünktlich (Termin:.........) □ Sofort □ | □ vollständig □ verständlich □ objektiv □ | □ Ordentlich zusammengefasst □ | □ Gar nicht □ Abgeordnet □ Im PC gespeichert □ |
| | | | □ Pünktlich (Termin:.........) □ Sofort □ | □ vollständig □ verständlich □ objektiv □ | □ Ordentlich zusammengefasst □ | □ Gar nicht □ Abgeordnet □ Im PC gespeichert □ |
| | | | □ Pünktlich (Termin:.........) □ Sofort □ | □ vollständig □ verständlich □ objektiv □ | □ Ordentlich zusammengefasst □ | □ Gar nicht □ Abgeordnet □ Im PC gespeichert □ |

## **2.2**

Irrelevante Informationen auf die Sie gerne verzichten wollen:

## 3. **Informationssicherheit**

3.1    Wie werden Lieferantendaten gespeichert?

Elektronisch oder auf Papier? Werden diesbezüglich irgendwelche Unterschiede gemacht (z.B. nur Adressen im Computer, Rest im Ordner)

Wie sichern Sie diese Daten gegen unbefugten Zugriff (Schlösser, Passwörter, Zugriffsbeschränkungen etc.)?

3.2    Wie werden Daten von Geschäftspartnern gespeichert?

Elektronisch oder auf Papier? Werden diesbezüglich irgendwelche Unterschiede gemacht (z.B. nur Adressen im Computer, Rest im Ordner)

Wie sicheren Sie diese Daten gegen unbefugten Zugriff (Schlösser, Passwörter, Zugriffsbeschränkungen etc.)?

3.3    Wie werden Daten der Buchhaltung/Finanzen gespeichert?

Elektronisch oder auf Papier? Werden diesbezüglich irgendwelche Unterschiede gemacht (z.B. nur Adressen im Computer, Rest im Ordner)

Wie sichern Sie diese Daten gegen unbefugten Zugriff (Schlösser, Passwörter, Zugriffsbeschränkungen etc.)?

3.4 Wie werde Kundendaten gespeichert(z.B. wenn sich ein Kunde beschwert und ihm nicht sofort geholfen werden kann)?
Elektronisch oder auf Papier?

Wie sichern Sie diese Daten gegen unbefugten Zugriff (Schlösser, Passwörter, Zugriffsbeschränkungen etc.)?

3.5 Wie werden Daten bezüglich des Sortiments (Bestelllisten etc.) gespeichert?
Elektronisch oder auf Papier?

Wie sichern Sie diese Daten gegen unbefugten Zugriff (Schlösser, Passwörter, Zugriffsbeschränkungen etc.)?

# 8 Literature

Books

Davenport, T. & Prusak, L. (1998). *Working Knowledge: How organization manage what they know.* Boston: Havard Business School Press.

De Wit, B. & Meyer, R. (2004). *Strategy: Process, Conent, Context: AN INTERNATIONAL PERSPECTIVE.* 3rd edition. London: Thomson Learning.

Eppler, M. (2003). *Managing Information Quality: Increasing the Value of Information in Knowledge-intensive Products and Processes.* Heidelberg: Springer Verlag Heidelberg Berlin.

Fank, M. (2001). *Einführung in das Informationsmanagement: Grundlagen, Methoden, Konzepte.* 2nd edition. Managementwissen für Studium und Praxis. München: Oldenbourg Wissenschaftsverlag GmbH.

Heinrich, L. & Lehner, F. (2005). *Informationsmanagement: Planung, Überwachung und Steuerung der Informationsinfrastruktur.* 8th edition. München: Oldenbourg Wissenschafts Verlag GmbH.

Hafner, M. (2005). *Entwicklung einer Methode für das Management der Informationssystemarchitektur im Unternehmen.* Dissertation. St. Gallen: Universität.

Heinzelbecker, K. (1985). *Marketing Informationssysteme.* Mainz: Verlag W. Kohlhammer GmbH.

Hildebrand, K. (2001). *Informationsmanagement: Wettbewerbsorientierte Informationsverarbeitung mit Standard Software und Internet.* 2nd edition. Lehr und Handbücher der Betrienbswirtschaftslehre. München: Oldenbourg Wissenschaftsverlag GmbH.

Horváth, P (1996). *Controlling.* 6th edition. München: Verlag Vahlen.

Krcmar, H. (2005). *Informationsmanagement.* 4th edition. Berlin: Springer Berlin Heidelberg New York.

Lincoln, T. (1990). *Managing Information Systems for profit.* In John Wiley Information Systems series. Chichester: John Wiley and Sons Ltd.

Königer, P. & Reithmayer, W. (1998). *Management unstrukturierter Informationen: Wie Unternehmen die Informationsflut beherrschen können.* Frakfurt/Main, New York: Campus Verlag.

Kroenke, D. & Hatch, R. (1994). *Management Information Systems.* 3rd edition. Watsonville: McGraw-Hill.

Link, J. (1982). *Die methodologischen, informationswirtschaftlichenund führungspolitischen Aspekte des Controlling.* Zeitschrift für Betriebswirtschaft 52(3). 261-280.

Murdick, G. (1980). *MIS: Concept and Design.* Englewood Cliffs: Prentice-Hall, Inc.

Nonaka, I. &Takeuchi, H. (1995). *The knowledge-creating company: How Japanese companies create the dynamics of innovation.* Oxford: Oxford University Press.

Schmolke, S. , Deitermann, M. & Rückwart, W. (2006). *Industrielles Rechnungswesen: Finanzbuchhaltung – Analyse und Kritik des Jahresabschlusses – Kosten- und Leistungsrechnung: Einführung in die Praxis.* 34th edition. Darmstadt: Bildungshaus SchulbuchverlageWestermann Schroedel Diesterweg Schöningh Winklers GmbH.

Schwarze, J. (1998). *Informationsmanagement: Planung, Steuerung, Koordination und Kontrolle der Informationsversorgung im Unternehmen.*

NWB-Studienbücher-Wirtschaftsinformatik. Herne/Berlin:Verlag Neue
Wirtschafts-Briefe GmbH & Co.

Shenk, D. (1997). *Datasmog- Surviving the Information Glut.* New York:
Harper Collins.

Wöhe, G. (2002). *Einführung in die allgemeine Betriebswirtschaftslehre.* 21st
edition. München: Verlag Vahlen.

Electronic

*Bürosysteme.*(2005). Microsoft® Encarta® 2006 [DVD]. Microsoft
Corporation.

Detsch, R. (2005). *Kosten.* Microsoft® Encarta® 2006 [DVD]. Microsoft
Corporation.

Habermeyer, W. (2005). *Information.* Microsoft® Encarta® 2006 [DVD].
Microsoft Corporation

*Informationswissenschaft.* (2005). Microsoft® Encarta® 2006 [DVD].
Microsoft Corporation.

Kraus, U. (2005). *Ertrag.* Microsoft® Encarta® 2006 [DVD]. Microsoft
Corporation.

Nettersheim, C. (2005). *Kommunikationswissenschaft.* Microsoft® Encarta®
2006 [DVD]. Microsoft Corporation.

Vierecke, A. (2005). *Kommunikation, soziale.* Microsoft® Encarta® 2006
[DVD]. Microsoft Corporation.

Internet

*Glossar der wichtigsten Begriffe der Evaluationsforschung.* [Internet]. Available from: <http://web.fu-berlin.de/eval-qs-qm/pdf/Glossar_Begriffe_der_Evaluationsforschung.pdf>. [05/06/2006].

The Marketing Teacher (2006). *Balanced Scorecard-Lesson.* [Internet]. Available from: <http://www.marketingteacher.com/Lessons/lesson_balanced_scorecard.htm>. [18/06/2006].

Scheiner, J. (2003). *Bewertungsverfahren in der Verkahrsplanung.*Raum und Mobilität: Arbeitspapiere des FachbgebietsVerkehrswesen und verkehrsplanung 9. Dortmund: Universität Dortmund.

Scholles, F. (2006). *6.4 Die Kosten-Nutzen-Analyse.* [Internet]. Available from: <http://www.laum.uni-hannover.de/ilr/lehre/Ptm/Ptm_Bew Kna.htm>. [27/05/2006].

Software-Engineering (2006). *Verfahren: Datenflussanalyse.* [Internet]. Available from: <http://www.software-kompetenz.de/?21059>. [03/06/2006].

Solution Matirx Ltd. (2006). *Kosten-Nutzen-Analyse.* [Internet]. Available from: <http://www.kostennutzenanalyse.de/?gclid=CLSA3qmg54UCFSlGM AodpmAnww>. [02/06/2006].

Wikipedia.org (2006). *Balanced Scorecard.* [Internet] Available from:<http://de.wikipedia.org/wiki/Balanced_Scorecard> [18/06/2006]

Wikipedia.org (2006). *Cost.* [Internet] Available from: <http://en.wikipedia.org/wiki/Communication> [27/06/2006].

Wikipedia.org (2006). *Communication.* [Internet] Available from:<http://en.wikipedia.org/wiki/Cost> [13/05/2006].

Wikipedia.org (2006). *Diskette*. [Internet] Available from:
<http://de.wikipedia.org/wiki/Diskette> [15/06/2006].

Wikipedia.org (2006). *Information*. [Internet] Available from:
<http://de.wiktionary.org/wiki/Information> [14/04/2006].

Wikipedia.org (2006). *Kommunikation*. [Internet] Available from:
<http://de.wikipedia.org/wiki/Kommunikation> [27/06/2006].

Wikipedia.org (2006). *Kosten-Nutzen-Analyse*. [Internet] Available from: <
http://de.wikipedia.org/wiki/Kosten-Nutzen-Analyse > [25/06/2006].

Wikipedia.org (2006). *Kosten-Wirksamkeits-Analyse*. [Internet] Available
from: <http://de.wikipedia.org/wiki/Kosten-Wirksamkeits-Analyse>
[25/06/2006].

Wikipedia.org (2006). *Management*. [Internet] Available from:
<http://de.wiktionary.org/wiki/Management> [14/05/2006].

Wikipedia.org (2006). *Nutzwertanalyse*. [Internet] Available from:
<http://de.wikipedia.org/wiki/Nutzwertanalyse> [25/06/2006].

Wikipedia.org (2006). *Oppotunitätskosten*. [Internet] Available from:
<http://de.wikipedia.org/wiki/Opportunit%C3%A4tskosten> [25/06/2006].

Wikipedia.org (2006). *Profit*. [Internet] Available from:
<http://en.wikipedia.org/wiki/Profit> [25/06/2006].

Wikipedia.org (2006). *USB-Stick*. [Internet] Available from:
<http://de.wikipedia.org/wiki/Usb-stick> [14/06/2006].

Scripts

Buric, K. (2003). *Wertorientiertes Informationsmanagement mit der Balanced Scorecard.* Hohenheim: Universität Hohenheim Fakultät Wirtschafts- und Sozialwissenschaften.

Merl, A. (2001). *Informationsmanagement als Basis einer marktbezogenen Unternehmensführung.* Available at <www.Hausarbeiten.de> [12/03/2006].

Runge, T. (2002). *Die Anwendung der Balanced Scorecard im Informationsmanagement.* Göttingen: Universität Göttingen.

Solbach, S. (1996). *Management Informationssysteme – Geschichte und Einführung von MIS.* Ravensburg: staatliche Berufsakademie.

University of Sunderland (2004). *Strategic Management of Human Resources.* Sunderland: University of Sunderland.

Personal Interviews

Mr. Oppel – CEO of art decor GmbH. [14/07/2006]

Mr. Kürbs – Sales Manager of art decor GmbH. [14/07/2006]

Mrs. Schönfeld – Accountant of art decor GmbH. [14/07/2006]

Mrs. Bösener – Chain Store Manager in Leipzig at art decor GmbH. [14/07/2006]

Mrs. Pleul – Chain Store Manager in Zwickau at art decor GmbH. [15/07/2006]

Mrs. Etzdorf – Chain Store Manager in Leipzig at art decor GmbH. [14/07/2006]

www.ingramcontent.com/pod-product-compliance
Lightning Source LLC
LaVergne TN
LVHW080103070326
832902LV00014B/2404